CONNIE'S DAHLIAS

A Beginner's Guide

Connie Thompson

Suite 300 - 990 Fort St
Victoria, BC, v8v 3K2
Canada

www.friesenpress.com

Copyright © 2021 by Connie Thompson
First Edition — 2021

All rights reserved.

No part of this publication may be reproduced in any form, or by any means, electronic or mechanical, including photocopying, recording, or any information browsing, storage, or retrieval system, without permission in writing from FriesenPress.

ISBN
978-1-03-910733-5 (Hardcover)
978-1-03-910732-8 (Paperback)
978-1-03-910734-2 (eBook)

1. *Gardening, Flowers, Annuals*

Distributed to the trade by The Ingram Book Company

Contents

ACKNOWLEDGEMENTS	**V**
GETTING STARTED	**1**
Where Do You Plan To Grow Your Dahlias?	1
BEFORE YOU PLANT	**7**
Early Spring	7
Starting Your Tubers Early To Get Early Blooms	9
PLANTING OUT TIME	**17**
Make The Weather Network Your Favorite Place To Visit!	17
Don't Rush To Planting	18
SUMMER DAHLIA CHORES	**23**
Pinching Out Or Stopping Your Dahlias	23
AND ONLY TOO SOON IT'S FALL!	**31**
Time To Dig Out Your Tubers	31
WINTER STORAGE	**35**
Zone 8 Or Higher	35
Zone 6 And Lower	36
Our Storage And Work Room	37
Okay, We Have The Storage Facility All Figured Out	39
SPLITTING YOUR DAHLIA TUBERS IN THE FALL	**41**
Getting Started With Splitting	41

QUESTIONS THAT I OFTEN GET FROM PEOPLE...	45
DAHLIA PESTS THAT WE ALL HAVE TO DEAL WITH	49
Slugs And Slug Bait Traps	49
Aphids	50
Wireworm	51
DAHLIA DISEASES	53
Leafy Gall	53
RESOURCE PAGE	57
ACKNOWLEDGEMENT PAGE	59

Acknowledgements

Growing dahlias is a truly rewarding experience. Dahlias are relatively easy to grow, and the blooms are amazing.

I would like to acknowledge my late father, J.E. Ted Underhill who started my interest in growing at an incredibly young age. He was published many times over the years.

I would also like to acknowledge my husband John, who is a huge help to me and allows me to still be actively growing in my mid-70s. Thank you for all that you do for me, and for how that allows us this wonderful opportunity to foster so much interest in growing dahlias.

I would also like to acknowledge my friend Karen Bull, who as a retired florist, taught me so much about making bouquets, corsages and boutonnieres that I do every summer for wedding work.

PHOTO CREDIT: My dear friend, Karen Bull

GETTING *Started*

WHERE DO YOU PLAN TO GROW YOUR DAHLIAS?

Before you start cultivating dahlias, you have to make sure that your garden is set up for success. That means deciding where you are going to plant. Do you have an existing garden that you can plant in? You will need loose soil where it is easy to dig down 10 inches. This is because the dahlia tubers need to be planted approximately five inches deep in the soil. Then, during the growing season, they produce many tubers that form quite a large clump. The soil needs to be loose enough that you can dig at least 10 inches deep in the fall to get the clumps out.

If the soil is compact and has a clay base, do not worry! You can still plant there. You just need to dig it over or rototill it to loosen it up. If you are digging up an existing lawn to make a dahlia bed, please remove the sod before you start rototilling to remove any grubs that may be lurking in that layer. You will have to rototill at least twice to get deep enough. I would add organic material at this time: compost, manure that does not have any herbicide lurking in the straw, leaves, etc.

You would be wise to get a PH kit from the nursery and check the PH levels of your soil. Dahlias like to be grown in soil with a PH between 6.7 to 6.8. If the PH is significantly lower than this, then your soil is too acidic. You can mix garden lime into your soil to raise the PH level.

Dahlias will tolerate a variety of climate zones, but they do not like extreme heat. If you live in Florida or Southern California, be prepared! Your dahlias will need some shade cloth or large umbrellas to get them through the hot spells. We use car shelter frames to mount shade cloth on, which has worked very well for us. Yes, dahlias are native to Mexico…..but up in the mountains were it is cooler and your not growing native species….your growing hybrids!

RAISED BEDS

Growing in raised beds is a great option for those with troublesome soil, particularly if you live on a hillside or slope, or have stony ground to deal with—which we do! Beds make planting and growing flowers quite easy.

Your bed should be 12 inches deep, with cardboard between the grass and the bed. There could be wireworms in your grass, and the cardboard will stop them from getting into the bed. (More information on this in the pest section near the back of the book.)

Over the past 12 years on the farm, my husband John and I have built 15 raised beds. Our favorite material to work with is landscape ties. I have been told these are readily available on the West Coast of Canada, as well as the East Coast. They are made from second-growth timber, cut four inches in diameter, and further sawn on two sides to make a flat surface on both sides to stack them. The ties come in eight-foot lengths and are pressure-treated. You can either drill and nail 10-inch galvanized nails through the ties, or you can screw the ties together with five-inch treated screws. This creates a bed that is 12 inches deep, four feet wide, and as long as you want it to be.

The last one John built was on a downward slope and 52 feet long. He started at the bottom, finding a level by digging into the ground to get the first course of ties in place. He then overlapped them as he went up the slope. The photo below will show you the finished product, and you can see how we dealt with the slope.

We have built these raised beds both east-west and north-south to best deal with the lay of the land. Because of our southern exposure, I see little difference in growth with either direction the beds are laying.

I have grown in raised beds for over 30 years, long before I met my husband, and would grow no other way now. They are wonderful to work in: you can control your soil, the fertilizer, and your watering with ease.

The photo below shows a good portion of our lower garden layout, showing both east-west and north-south beds. The metal uprights you can see are shelter frames that we cover with shade cloth during the heat of summer. We face due south and have full sunshine from sun-up to sun-down, and it can get extremely hot for the smaller blooms.

ORDERING YOUR DAHLIA TUBERS

Dahlias are not frost-tolerant. **Every fall you will have to dig the bulbs up, store them for the winter, and then replant them next spring.** Before you start growing, you need to think about where you will store them for the winter. Depending on how many dahlias you grow, they can take up quite a bit of space. More about this further in the book.

Late fall is your best time to order stock for the following year, as that is when most of the dahlia sites open for sale. Dahliaddict.com is a wonderful resource for available dahlias in North America, especially if you live in the U.S. Not all suppliers ship to Canada or export.

Please know that there is no such thing as 'dahlias for beginners.' Even if you are new to growing, they are easy to grow. I might suggest smaller blooms the first year, as they will bloom earlier and make wonderful cut flowers.

Local Dahlia Society tuber sales happen each spring—generally in late April—and are a wonderful resource. You can also trade dahlia tubers through trading sites on Facebook if you want to try a new variety. For those of you who have only grown nursery-variety dahlias, you have not experienced the wonderful dahlias that are hybridized in North America and recognized and sought around the world by growers.

Try to always grow good quality varieties—you will have fewer problems with diseases.

WOW—some tubers cost $10 each. Why? There is a ton of work involved in producing decent tubers. Expect to pay $7 to $10 per tuber, if not more. Remember, dahlia tubers are not cold hardy. They must be dug up by hand, and because they are quite fragile, they can break easily. If broken near the neck of the tuber, they will not grow. Hand digging is the gentlest method to get them out of the ground with the least amount of breakage, but it is HARD MANUAL LABOR. Once dug, they must be cleaned, trimmed up, and split by hand.

If you wait until spring to try to find dahlia tubers, most places will be sold out.

PREPARING YOUR DAHLIA BEDS

All soil needs amending, yearly, with organic material. Add well-aged manure, making sure it has not been treated with herbicide, especially the straw. Herbicide residue will affect your tubers for several years. Consider using:

- leaves—composted, or fresh as they fall from the trees every Fall.
- seaweed
- fish compost
- organic compost

You should also have your soil tested every couple of years. A routine soil test provides an in-depth description of the availability of nutrients for plant uptake that are in your soil. Years and years of putting chemical fertilizers on your soil can be problematic. The phosphorus and potassium in NPK fertilizers build up in your soil to the point that plants cannot access the nutrients they need anymore. With regular testing, you know what your soil requires and can rectify your soil's problems. There are many labs that will provide this service for a nominal cost; you can also try your local university's agricultural department.

CONNIE'S DAHLIAS

Last year, we had our soil tested and discovered that our phosphorus and potassium levels were way too high, which I had been suspicious of. Remediating an imbalance like that can take a couple of seasons.

Fall, right after digging out your tubers, is an excellent time to add manure. January is the best time to add garden lime if your PH shows that your soil is too acidic. Do not forget you want to aim for a PH of 6.7 to 6.8. If your PH is too low, your dahlias will struggle. You can get a PH kit at any good nursery.

If you have had a recent soil test and it shows your magnesium is low, you can use dolomite lime, which is a slow-release formula that includes magnesium instead of basic garden lime.

BEFORE You Plant

EARLY SPRING

Lay out your dahlia beds on graph paper, remembering height, color, plant size (most dahlias will make a plant 24 to 30 inches in diameter by the end of summer), and bloom size. Keep clear records and label your plants with the name of the variety. If you do not do this, you could have a six-foot dahlia growing in front of a three-foot one, and the shorter flower will get poor light. If that happens, you will not be able to enjoy the blooms come summertime.

Tags to label your plants can be purchased, or you can make them out of a Venetian blind cut to six inches in length and hole punched. I use a Pentel N50 marker, guaranteed not to fade in the sun for three years, which I buy online. Attach your tags to a garden stake with a cable tie or a piece of plastic-covered wire like electricians' wire.

For garden stakes we use rebar (construction steel), but you can use wood stakes, remembering that they will rot within a couple of years, or tall tomato cages placed over the planted tubers. If you use stakes, they need to be five to six feet tall and hammered into your soil until they hit the firm bottom of the bed. If you have loose soil, some of them can hammer in several feet. Stakes will give you a way to support your dahlia plants once they are fifteen to eighteen inches tall, and every fifteen inches after that.

Place your garden stakes where you plan to plant your tubers. For smaller blooms you can put in a stake every 28 inches, and plant one tuber on either side of that stake.

Dahlias need to be supported—they are basically a green tube full of water and foliage, and eventually flowers. If you get wind or rain during the summer and they are not supported, they can fall over and break off right at ground level. Remember, many dahlias grow five to seven feet tall, or more. Even when supported, sometimes when you get rain, the blooms fill up with water and break under the weight. Be prepared to do lots of deadheading to cut off these broken blooms every time you get rain.

WHEN YOUR TUBER ORDER ARRIVES

Your tuber orders are arriving! **Be sure to unpack them and check the tubers to make sure there is no sign of a broken tuber or mold.** Notify your supplier if you see either of these problems, as they are responsible for replacing them. If your tubers arrive more than three weeks before you can safely plant in your area, please re-pack them and put them in a cool spot (where they will not freeze!) until you want to start waking them up. That should be done two to three weeks prior to planting directly into the ground.

Remember, there are two things necessary for a viable tuber:

1. The tuber MUST have at least one eye, which only appears at the crown or top of the tuber. Eyes will never appear on the side or the root-end of a tuber.

    a   The eye is where the sprout will grow (like a potato that has been in the bag too long). These tubers have been stored dormant for the winter, and it can be difficult to see an eye when they first arrive and have not been introduced to warmth.

    b   If you have two or three eyes on one tuber that is okay, but you will also have two or three stalks instead of one strong central stalk. When closer to planting time, you can safely remove the skinny sprout(s) and grow with the strongest one. This will ensure you have a strong central stock for the summer.

2. The neck MUST be intact. If it is broken or damaged, the tuber is worthless. If you purchase tubers from big-box locations, they are Dutch imports and will have lots of broken or damaged tubers. Remove them and keep the solid tubers that are attached to the crown.

Be sure to keep good records and label your plants with the name of the variety. I write on all my tubers with a black Sharpie marker. This saves a lot of guessing later in the season when you cannot remember the name! After you have dug it out in the fall, you might still be able to see the name of the mother tuber—if it has not rotted during the growing season, which can happen.

Remember, when your tubers arrive, you may or may not already be able to see the eye or eyes. The photo below has them circled so you know what you are looking for.

STARTING YOUR TUBERS EARLY TO GET EARLY BLOOMS

. . . if this is what you want to do.

To do this successfully, you will need to be properly set up. That means a greenhouse heated to 70° F or 72° F, or indoors where it is warm, and you have enough space. If you start your tubers early, you will be five or six weeks ahead of the game and have early blooms as a result.

Remember, if you plant bare root tubers in the ground at planting time (tubers that are not sprouted), they will take three to five weeks, or more, just to sprout. Sprouting takes a combination of potting soil, warmth, and moisture. It also takes good light, and I do **not** mean next to your window. You need fluorescent or LED bars of lights mounted within 10 inches of your sprouting tubers.

Timing is especially important; you do not want to start them too early if you do not have proper lighting. They will get leggy amazingly fast searching for light if you are just depending on window light.

If you wish to do this for a head start and have the room and set-up to do so, you can start to 'wake up your tubers' six to eight weeks prior to planting time. To start, you need a tray, and I recommend the 11-by-22-inch standard trays available at nurseries. Buy a tall clear plastic dome with a vent in the top or cover the tray loosely with a piece of bubble wrap. You are just trying to keep the moisture level even during the process, and this will be your 'nursery' to wake up your tubers.

Remember to write the name of the variety on each tuber with a Sharpie marker!

Put some potting soil or potting soil mixed with vermiculite, coarse sand, or wood shavings, roughly three-quarters of an inch deep, in your tray. Lay your tubers on top of this, then sprinkle more potting soil mix over to cover them. They should be covered pretty much up to the crown end where the tuber eyes will sprout.

Make sure that the potting soil is evenly moist, but not wet.

Put the clear dome over the top, with the vents open, or lay a piece of bubble wrap over the tray and keep it in a warm spot in your house. A house temperature of about 70° F to 72° F will be fine. Waking up the tubers will take three to five weeks before you can expect to see sprouts. They do not all sprout at the same time.

At this stage of the game, they need warmth. They do not need lights until they have sprouted. Have a spray bottle full of water ready, and as the soil starts to dry out, mist them lightly so the soil remains moist all the time.

Once they have sprouted with a one-inch sprout, it is time to pot them up. It is NOT necessary to use a one-gallon pot for this. I use three-inch pots because they fit in my trays and make sure that the tuber can sit in them, often at an angle. I prefer small tubers to grow from, as they start producing roots faster rather than just living off a fat tuber full of starch reserves.

If the only tuber you have available is larger, use a slightly larger pot, one that is big enough for the tuber and enough potting soil to cover up to the top of the crown of the dahlia, where the sprout is. Cover the sprout slightly.

If your tuber is long, cut it to fit in your pot, allow the cuts to dry for 24 hours, then pot them up.

You can see the crown of the tuber in this photo—please cover it so that there is at least one-quarter of an inch of potting soil over it. When it is planting time, it will get covered along with the sprout. More on this further on.

TAKING CUTTINGS FROM YOUR TUBERS TO INCREASE TUBER STOCK

This is an excellent way to increase your stock if you only have one tuber available and would like more. The surest way to increase stock is by either producing more tubers or taking cuttings.

To take cuttings, you need to wake up the tubers that you wish to take cuttings from roughly 10 to 12 weeks before your planting time. These tubers will take three to five weeks to sprout. The tubers will take another three weeks to grow the sprout enough to take the cutting, then another two weeks to make a root system. They will then take another three or four weeks to grow, then harden off before planting in your garden. There are a lot of variables in the timing of this, as you can see, but it is a roughly 10-week process.

Lay up the tubers that you wish to take cuttings from in the same way you would if you were starting early. When they have a half-inch sprout or more, take them out of the 'nursery' tray and pot them up in a three-inch pot. Grow them until they have a roughly three-inch sprout to make your cut.

Get them under lights right away so they do not get 'leggy;' having them on a heat mat during the day will speed up the process. If you are using a heat mat and do not have a thermostat, you might want to put something between the heat mat and the tray you are starting them in, for instance, a couple of those strong trays you get at nurseries with big holes in them. That will give you a bit of a barrier, so the tubers do not get too hot. If you are lucky, your tuber might have two or three eyes, and you can take more cuttings.

When your shoots are approximately three to three-and-a-half inches long, it is time to take your cuttings. You need to be prepared for this with another tray, with two-inch pots filled with sterile potting or seedling soil that is not too heavy. You will also need a clear dome with vents to put over your tray, with the vents open. If your pots have been used before, wash them, and then do a bleach rinse to kill any spores.

You will need labels to put the variety name into each cutting pot, preferably with a Pentel N50 marker to make sure the ink does not fade under the lights. You will also need rooting powder, or rooting gel, and a razor or scalpel to take the cuttings with. In addition, you will need a pencil to make a hole in the soil in each two-inch pot and a container with 10 percent bleach solution in it to dip your razor or scalpel in between each cut.

With your scalpel, cut off your first cutting, leaving one-eighth of an inch of the sprout on the tuber. Four more 'starts' will appear within a couple of days, which will be the start of your next few cuttings. The photo below shows you where to make your cuts.

In the photo above, you can see that I suggest removing the two bottom leaves close to the stalk without cutting the stalk. You also need to remove about 50 percent of the top leaves, as shown. There is just too much foliage there for a cutting to support while it is making roots.

After dipping the cutting in a rooting hormone (if you like to use one), put the cutting into the sterile mix, deep enough to cover the leaf node where the bottom set of leaves were.

Put a label with the variety name into each pot and, after dipping the cutting into your rooting medium, carefully place it into the hole you have made in the soil. Press down around the stalk.

Put these two-inch pots with their cuttings into the tray, and make sure they are quite moist but not wet. Cover them with the clear dome with vents open and place the whole tray on the shelf under the lights and on a heat mat if you have one. Then watch the magic happen. (If you are using fluorescent light bars, a heat mat will not be necessary as they give off enough heat on their own.)

Within 10 to 14 days, you should start to see roots showing in the holes at the bottom of the pot. If they have not started after two weeks, give them a few more days. Make sure that there is lots of humidity under that dome, but not dripping wet. When you can see the first of the roots, it is time to transplant the cuttings into three-inch pots, with fresh sterile potting soil, in a tray under the lights. The roots will not happen all happen at once; just keep an eye on them. It is quite normal to lose a few to 'damping off.'

Keep a dome on them for a couple more days, then remove it and leave them under lights, which should be on for 14 to 16 hours a day.

Within roughly three weeks your cuttings will be ready to harden off, but make sure that they have three or four pairs of leaves before you do this. They will need constant light until they can go outside to your greenhouse or on a table if your nighttime temperatures are warm enough. You do not want them outside if your overnight temps drop below 50° F. Remember, these are new cuttings!

MAKE YOUR OWN GROWING BOOTH—EASY TO SET UP AND STORE

I have a PVC shelving unit that is available at most large hardware outlets for about $28. I mounted grow lights on the underside of each shelf with cable ties to make an easy, homemade growing booth. One light bar per shelf will give adequate light, and it needs to be on for 14 to 16 hours a day. My shelf unit is 30 inches wide, so I bought three

24-inch LED light bars, and I get plenty of light from them. I use three shelves every year for either growing or making cuttings.

Because I use this each year, I have covered the outside of the shelf unit with a roll of foil insulation wrap, the kind that you would put around a hot water tank. I taped it on with a roll of the foil tape that comes with the insulation wrap. This keeps the warmth from the lights in the shelf unit and stops light from escaping out the back or sides. I also put a piece of something on top of the top shelf to stop heat/light from escaping from there.

HARDENING YOUR PLANTS

When this work is finished and you have nice-looking young dahlia plants, it is time to harden them off. If it is warm enough outside to put your potted tubers in your greenhouse before planting out, this would be an ideal spot. If you do not have a greenhouse, find a sheltered place outside about a week prior to planting out time, and let them get used to the day and night temperatures.

Your shelf unit can be taken apart for storage along with your light bars. Mine lives outside one of the outside doors on our farm, and never gets taken apart anymore. This saves us from having to put the foil back on every spring.

Because we grow so many dahlias, once the tubers are potted up and growing, they get moved into our greenhouse. This is usually the first week of March. The tables in our greenhouse are fitted with heating cables with two inches of sand on top, which makes a large radiant heated surface on each table. It is still early March when we do this, and we can still have rather cool night temperatures, so the tables are set up with four-inch screws drilled into two sides of each table, and hoops of black five-eighth-inch drip irrigation pipe cut to make hoops that go over the screws and over each bed.

These are draped with clear plastic over the top, day and night, and frost cloth over that every night as well. You might have to use clothes pegs or something like them to fasten the clear plastic and stop it from sliding off. If it is a particularly cool night, we also put a covering of polyester fiberfill over the top. This gets them through those first few weeks, and by the end of March they can be grown with just the plastic over the top at night. We roll the plastic sheeting back for the daytime hours, as the heat can build up under it quite fast.

We can generally plant here by the third week of April when the plants have three to seven sets of leaves. Our climate is very temperate, similar to northern coastal Washington.

Though this might seem over-the-top for many new growers, it might help someone down the road as they increase their growing stock. The photo below was taken in early April, but you can still see the hoops. We do not need to cover them at all by mid-April. The heating cables are still on every day for a couple of weeks in the early part of the month, and that is enough heat for them. Be prepared for regular misting, as they will dry out quickly.

The heating cables increase the inside temperature of the plastic-covered greenhouse by quite a few degrees, depending, of course, on the overnight temperature. But in the five or six years we have been starting them this way, we have never lost a plant or tuber to freezing.

EARWIG TRAPS

When your garden stakes are in place, it is a good time to put out your earwig traps. Earwigs do a lot of damage to your flowers; they like to visit at night and nibble on the petals. There are a couple of things that you can do to combat them, and it is best to do this about the time you plant.

Save small cat food or tuna fish tins and fill them with canola oil. Put one under each dahlia plant. The earwigs are attracted to the oil and will drown.

You can also make earwig traps like my photo below. I purchase 50-foot rolls of three-eighth inch inside diameter soaker hose, cut into seven-inch lengths. Using plastic clothes pegs purchased at the dollar store, fasten the hose pieces to the stake at roughly the same height as the flowers will be.

Have a bucket of soapy water available, and every few days, remove the piece of soaker hose and tap it into the bucket of soapy water. Make sure both ends of the hose are open.

You will catch thousands of earwigs this way and have flowers in much better condition.

If your having problems with ants, mix up a mixture of runny jam or excess canned fruit with a teaspoon of BORAX in small containers and put around the base of your dahlias. The ants will crawl in, eat it and die in the can.

PLANTING
Out time

MAKE THE WEATHER NETWORK YOUR FAVORITE PLACE TO VISIT!

Your dahlias can be planted in prepared soil as soon as the soil temperature is 55° F to 60° F (or 12° C to 15° C), and overnight temperatures are well above freezing.

Please keep a good eye on your weather for the next few weeks before you plant. You do not want to have weather ruin all your hard work!

Tubers planted directly into the ground rather than pre-starting can take a cool night better than a sprouted tuber with the growth. You do not want a week of rain after you plant them. If you know heavy rain is on the way, WAIT until it has passed, and the ground has had a couple of days to drain before planting.

Make the weatherman your best friend when you grow dahlias, especially around planting time!

— Diagram 'Fahrenheit to Celsius conversion chart'

Fahrenheit/Celsius Conversion Table

°C	°F
	-4
-20	5
-15	14
-10	23
15	32
0	41
5	50
10	59
15	68
20	77
25	86
30	95
35	104
40	

CONNIE THOMPSON

DON'T RUSH TO PLANTING

If your soil is cold and wet, they will just sit there—and probably rot! I see too many people impatient to get their tubers in the ground without checking the weather. Temperature is important, too. You do not want nighttime temps dropping below 40° F. You are just taking too much of a chance. Ideally, 50° F overnight to plant out is perfect.

PLEASE DO NOT pinch them out before you plant out your pre-started tubers in the ground. Remember, when you plant out, you generally put them into a five-inch-deep hole and often cover the bottom set of leaves, or perhaps two sets if you have pre-started your tubers. More on this to follow.

STAKING REVIEW

Let us review important information about staking to make sure you have not missed anything!

- Any dahlia that grows over three feet tall requires a stake. It also allows for a straighter, more beautiful plant.
- We use rebar stakes, but you can use cedar or even bamboo for small blooms.
- Pound in your stakes. If you have loose soil, your stake could pound in up to two feet.
- Tie your ties to the stake first, and then around the plant when it reaches roughly two feet in height, then every fifteen inches after that.

Many dahlias attain four-and-a-half to six feet in height. I recommend that you put your stakes in before you plant, so you do not DRIVE THE STAKE into the tubers!

OKAY, SO YOU KNOW WHAT THE WEATHER IS DOING AND YOU'RE READY TO PLANT

Your garden stakes are in place, your labels are made up, and you are ready to go.

Carefully dig a hole about eight inches away from both sides of your garden stakes, five inches deep and . . .

1. If you are planting a bare root tuber, lay it in the bottom of the hole and cover with two inches of soil. When the tuber finally sprouts—remember, three to five weeks and the sprout finally appears above the soil level—then you can slowly back-fill the hole with soil, covering the sprout until the hole is level with the surrounding ground. You want the warmth of the sun to stimulate the tuber

to grow—that is why you do not bury it right away. Make sure that your soil is moist but not wet, and do not let it dry out!

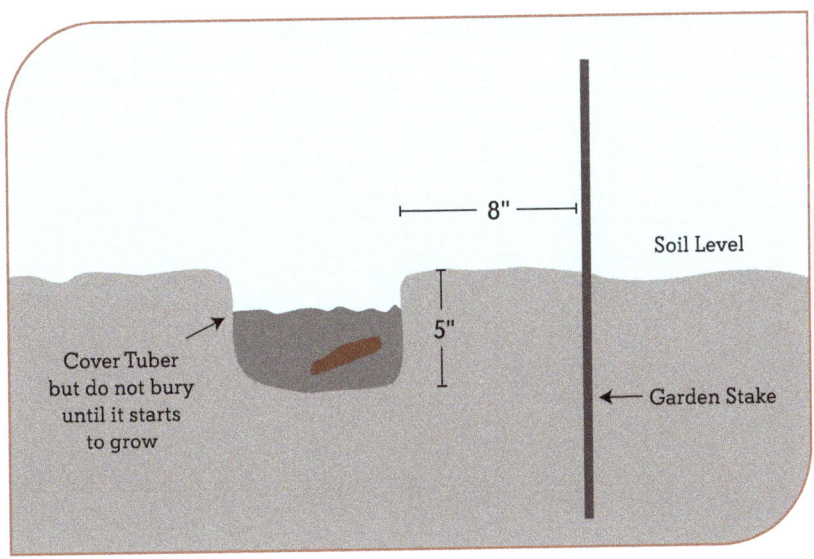

Diagram 'Planting a bare root tuber'

2. If you are planting a pre-started tuber, knock it out of the pot carefully so as not to disturb the roots too much. Place the small, rooted dahlia in the bottom of the hole and back-fill. If the tuber already has several sets or pairs of leaves, you might want to cover the bottom one or two sets of leaves. It is not necessary to fill all the soil in this hole until the plant has grown more, but I would cover the first set of leaves, at least at this point.

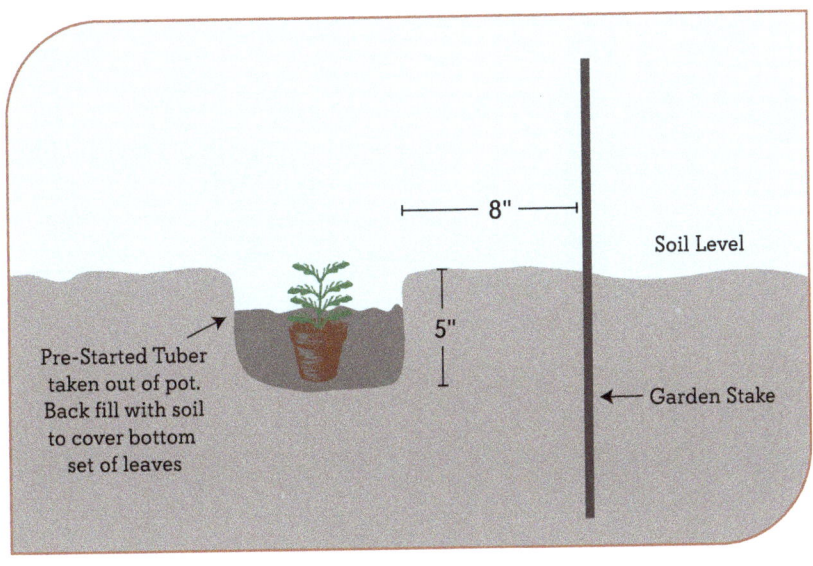

Diagram 'Planting a potted tuber in a hole'

Spacing is generally done according to the size of the plant and the blooms. We plant all small blooms (under six inches in diameter) on a 12-inch grid, but the average garden would space this size 15 to 18 inches apart.

All giant bloom varieties (over six inches in diameter) require more room. This includes all varieties with blooms from eight to 12 inches in diameter. These varieties can become rather LARGE plants, and you could safely plant one or two plants every 30 inches in your garden beds.

FERTILIZING

How you fertilize depends on whether you are planting dry root tubers or pre-started tubers.

IF YOU ARE PLANTING DRY ROOT TUBERS: When you are planted, I would go back over the garden and fertilize with a balanced fertilizer (8-8-8 or 10-10-10) to get the plants growing. It is not necessary to put it in the bottom of the hole—fertilizers work with root systems, and by the time your tuber has made a root system, the fertilizer will have worked itself into your soil. If you are expecting a light spring rain, it will start taking the fertilizer into the ground.

IF YOU ARE PLANTING PRE-STARTED TUBERS: In this case, use the same fertilizer but in the bottom of the hole, and brush a bit of soil over the fertilizer before planting your pre-started tubers to not burn the fragile root system.

AN ALTERNATIVE would be one handful of Alfalfa pellets in the bottom of each hole. Dahlias love Alfalfa! It would be the best alternative if you have not had a SOIL TEST in the past two years.

WATERING

If the soil is moist already, do not water it, but if the soil is bone dry, water lightly. Keep a good eye on the young plants over the next few weeks! Do not let them dry out. Again, if you are getting a bit of spring rain, that will be enough moisture.

The trick is to keep the soil moist, but never wet. Dahlias do not need a lot of water until they are established!

WATCH THE MAGIC

Now you can sit back and watch what is happening. Three to five weeks after planting bare root tubers, you will start to see them poking their sprouts through the soil. If you planted pre-started tubers, they would start to grow quickly. They will not need fertilizer again until they are a good 12 inches out of the ground.

Dahlias do not like mulch—besides, it is a great place for bugs to hide that want to eat your plants! However, I know many people in hot climates use it.

GROWING IN CONTAINERS

Not everyone has a garden area large enough to grow their dahlias in the ground. These people can grow in a container. BE SURE TO USE LARGE ONES, at least 15 inches or more across. One planted tuber can make a huge clump by fall that pretty much fills that container.

All dahlias grown in pots will require more care, more staking, MORE WATER, and more fertilizer. Please use light-colored pots, as black pots attract heat, and your dahlias will be miserable.

I would suggest staking with tomato cages—tall ones for sure if your plant is a tall variety over three-and-a-half feet.

When the weather gets warm you will be watering every day and if HOT, twice a day.

Please do not place these pots against the wall of your house or a solid fence-line, especially if it is made from concrete. The heat shining on concrete increases the temperature in your pots by a huge amount. It is basically frying them in the pots, and the plant will spend the summer leaning away from that heat. They will be much happier if the pots are grown out in the open or on a deck away from walls.

SUMMER
Dahlia Chores

PINCHING OUT OR STOPPING YOUR DAHLIAS

After you have planted and the plants are growing roughly eight to 10 inches out of the ground, it is time to Pinch Out your plants (also known as stopping the 'Terminal Growth'). Both terms are extensively used as dahlia terminology. (This has nothing to do with lengthening your stems…..that is 'Disbudding….. more later..')

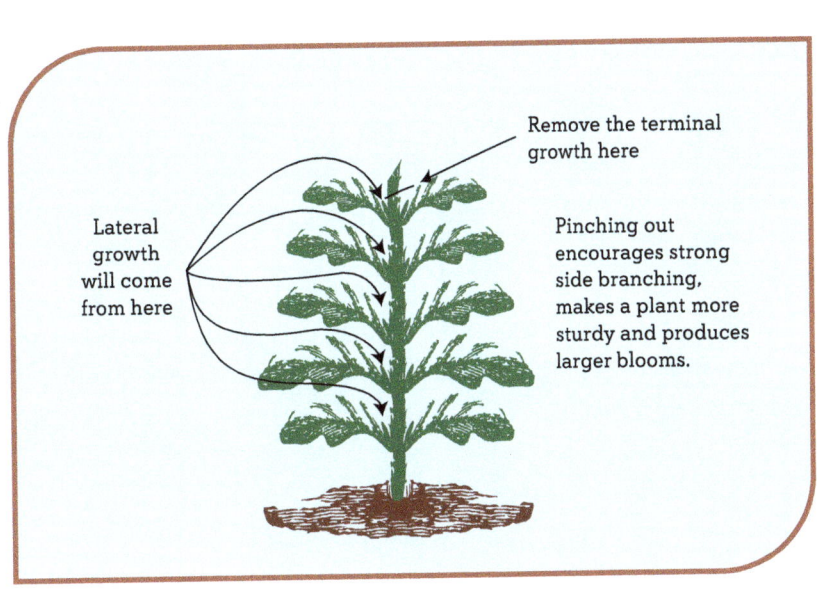

Diagram 'Pinching of the Terminal Bud'

This is only done one time per season and will stimulate your plants to start branching out and making more lateral growth. That provides you with a sturdy, lush plant, and ultimately more blooms. We all want more blooms! If you pinch out properly, you will quickly see new growth shoots coming from where every leaf node is attached to the stalk. This is where all those wonderful blooms will come from.

If you do not pinch out, the plant will continue to send the 'Terminal Growth' upwards until it finally gets tall enough to produce one bloom. When that one is cut off, then it will start to make laterals. You will have lost weeks of lateral growth (and many blooms!) as a result.

Approximately 60 days after pinching out, you should see your first blooms.

FERTILIZER—ROUND TWO

When your plants are roughly one foot tall, they get their second application of fertilizer. Dahlias are heavy feeders and need feeding approximately every four weeks. Again, I stress having your SOIL TESTED every couple of years. It is important to know what your soil is lacking or has too much of already, especially if this is a new garden to you, and you do not know the components of your soil.

NPK Fertilizers: The numbers on your fertilizer (like 10-10-10) measure the percentage of each nutrient that fertilizer provides. NITROGEN is the first number, PHOSPHORUS is the middle number, and POTASSIUM (potash) is the third number. So 10-10-10 means 10% nitrogen, 10% phosphorus, and 10% potassium.

Nitrogen promotes growth and provides lush foliage; it does not store in the ground and needs to be applied every year. We use UREA here at the farm, about two weeks prior to planting. 45-0-0 is the NPK number for this product. We get a ton of rain each year and it gets washed out quickly. Our soil test results that we got the other day indicate that we need LOTS of nitrogen this coming spring!

Phosphorus promotes blooms and strong root growth. This substance builds in your soil, so do not add a lot unless your soil requires it. Water does not wash it away, and it can remain in your soil for two to three years. When your phosphorus amounts get too high, it can 'lock up' your soil's ability to take up nutrients.

Potassium (potash) builds good tubers and builds up in your soil.

MYTH—Some people say that dahlias do not need nitrogen—this is totally wrong! All plants need nitrogen to flourish. What you need to know is not to give them nitrogen after mid-August, or you could have storage problems.

RABBIT PROBLEMS—EATING YOUR YOUNG DAHLIAS

This is a problem for many people in North America. I saw a suggestion a year or so ago about purchasing mesh garbage baskets or laundry baskets from your local dollar store and putting them over your young dahlia plants. Once they have grown to the height of the basket, they have grown large enough to withstand a bit of nibbling.

People have told me that they work well with a rock or a brick on top to keep the basket or container upright! You would need a container with roughly 15 inches of headroom.

TYING UP YOUR DAHLIAS

When your plants are about 15 inches or more out of the ground, you should start to support them. Tie your tie around the stake (not the plant) and then around the plant, carefully, so they do not fall over or get knocked over.

We grow in raised beds and have problems with deer walking through the beds. I peripheral tie all our beds to keep them from doing this as soon as I plant. Deer hooves can do a lot of damage. So can dogs and cats—be aware of this.

I start in one corner of each bed and wrap the perimeter tie around each stake until I have gone around the entire bed. This is repeated at 15 to 18-inch intervals in height. In our case, it keeps deer from walking through the beds and breaking the young plants. It also keeps our poodle from jumping into the beds to chase the cat and break plants.

I tie very few individual plants unless they are very tall and leaning. Instead, I crosstie through the beds so that four or five plants grow in a restricted area. To tie over 700 individual plants would require hired help!

Continue to tie up every 15 inches in height until you reach the top of your stakes. If you are growing in tall tomato cages, the cage will do this work for you.

I use a nylon material called NYLOTEX: it lasts for years and will not rot. It is a nylon material that people have used to make mats out of for years and does not damage the stalks. We store it in buckets for the off-season with holes in the bottom. I have found it on the internet and sometimes find it in our local thrift shops. Best stuff that I have ever found for tying dahlias, and in my 30 years of growing I've tried at lot of different things.

MAINTENANCE

Check your dahlias regularly for tying up and weeding, as necessary. If you have pre-started dahlias, after they have been growing in the ground for three or four weeks, you will start to see early flower buds. **It is important to remove these early buds—you want your plants to be concentrating on growing taller and filling out, not making flowers at this point.** The next flush of buds is okay to leave on the plants. Flowers about 60 days away!

If you planted bare root tubers, check them after a month or so to see if they are showing signs of sprouts. If you are digging about, do it gently or you could break off the sprout . . . PATIENCE!

Keep an eye on the moisture level in your soil, you do not want it to dry out. Dahlias need moisture to sprout and grow, but they do not want to either dry out or be in wet soil until well-established.

When your plants are 12 to 14 inches tall, it is time for their next fertilizing. If you have access to OSMOCOTE 14-14-14, it is very handy. This time-released fertilizer gives your plants fertilizer for the whole summer. It is not necessary to fertilize after mid-August, as this can impede storage ability for the winter, particularly a fertilizer with nitrogen.

An alternative would be using a Seaweed Concentrate on your plants. I use this all summer long and am very pleased with the results.

This is also a good time to check your labels and make sure they are still legible, so you'll know the name of your variety when it's time to dig out and store for the winter.

DEADHEADING

Once your plants are actively growing and making blooms, it is important to deadhead them. When fully double blooms show their pollen center, it is time to remove the bloom. Deadheading stimulates the plants to produce the next flush of blooms. Cut the branch down to just above the next set of leaves, where the next pair of buds will be forming.

If you do not do this regularly, the plant will think it has stopped producing flowers for the summer, and you will get fewer and fewer new blooms.

The photo below will help you understand when to deadhead your flowers. The bloom circled in RED shows a bloom that is at the perfect stage of growth to cut your blooms. The bloom that is circled in TURQUOISE shows a bloom that has a Blown Center, with the yellow pollen center exposed. It needs to be removed to stimulate your plant to make the next flush of blooms.

DISBUDDING YOUR DAHLIAS TO GET LONGER STEMS

I also need to explain DISBUDDING to you, so you can get a longer stem if you like to cut blooms. Some varieties naturally make long stems, but too many of them make noticeably short stems that are awful for trying to use as a cut flower. You want stems that are 14 to 16 inches long for this purpose.

You will see in the photo below that there are three buds that form the central growth, the MAIN FLOWER BUD and two side-buds that get removed. This way, you will get a longer stem to cut, and the main flower will be noticeably larger as a result. If you do not do this, you will get all three blooms with six to eight-inch stems. With some varieties that produce noticeably short stems, I would also remove the bud starts at the next leaf node down before it has a chance to become larger. Yes, you will lose some blooms, but you will have a bigger bloom and nice straight stems to cut.

We grow more than 700 dahlia plants every summer. I spend all summer long disbudding, for an hour or two every day. This keeps the plants producing decent-length stems to cut when I need them for bouquets or wedding work.

SUMMER WATERING

When the weather starts to really warm up, you need to do regular watering. We regularly water during July and August, every other day, for 15 to 20 minutes per bed; in June, we water as necessary, as our June can be damp. If we have a temperature spike into the high 80s or 90s F, we water daily. This is stressful for dahlias, as the heat inhibits the dahlias' ability to get vital nutrients.

After a hot spell, I give each dahlia plant a tablespoon of Epson salts, which is magnesium sulfate, and water it in well. You will notice a huge improvement in the appearance of your dahlias within roughly 24 hours, and the leaves will green quickly. Do not do it too often, but once or twice a summer when it has been HOT, the plants will benefit from it.

STRIPPING YOUR PLANTS

In mid-August, I strip the lower leaves off all the dahlia plants. They get stripped about 10 inches up the stalk from the soil level. This provides decent airflow during hot August and September weather and will generally help ensure you have less powdery mildew. We get little, if any, by doing this every summer.

In my photo below, you can see the white tags I make from Venetian blinds close to the soil-level cable tied around each dahlia stalk. With the lower leaves removed, not only do the plants get better airflow, but I can also reach in and remove all sorts of weeds and debris. It is nice when it becomes digging out time in the fall that this job is done.

AND ONLY
Too soon it's fall!

TIME TO DIG OUT YOUR TUBERS

Depending on where you are located, you could be thinking about cutting back and digging out your dahlias by mid-to-late September. It is important to plan this next step, as dahlia storage is so important. Because of our heavy November rains, which can rot dahlias in the ground, we start to cut down October 1st every year. We have over 700 plants to cut down, dig out, split, and label. This takes us about five weeks each year.

Remember, once dahlias have been growing in the ground for four months (or 120 days), they are mature enough to store for the winter. It is important that you have a good storage place that's cool, secure, and rodent proof!

MYTH: You do not have to wait for a hard frost and blackening of the foliage before you cut them down and dig them out. This is an old wives' tale that has been perpetuated by too many people for far too long!

Do this job on YOUR timetable, one that suits your location.

You need to know when your **Last Frost Date** is in the spring so that you can plan your planting, and the **First Frost Date** in the fall so you can get them out before they turn to mush and slime. This information will help you with both planting timing and dig out timing. Do a little research for this information for your location.

Knowing this information lets you decide that you might want to start your tubers early if your growing season is short. This way, they are actively growing when you plant the tubers, which gives them enough time to mature and bloom before it is time to get them out in the fall. Starting your tubers early buys you about five or six more weeks of growing time.

GROWING ZONES IN NORTH AMERICA

You will note that most growing zones are shared by both the US and Canada on both coasts! Zone 7b, for instance, which is the zone that I live in on the east coast of Vancouver Island, British Columbia, extends down the west coast of the US and across the southern states to the eastern seaboard. **Your Growing Zone is NOT distinctive to just your area.**

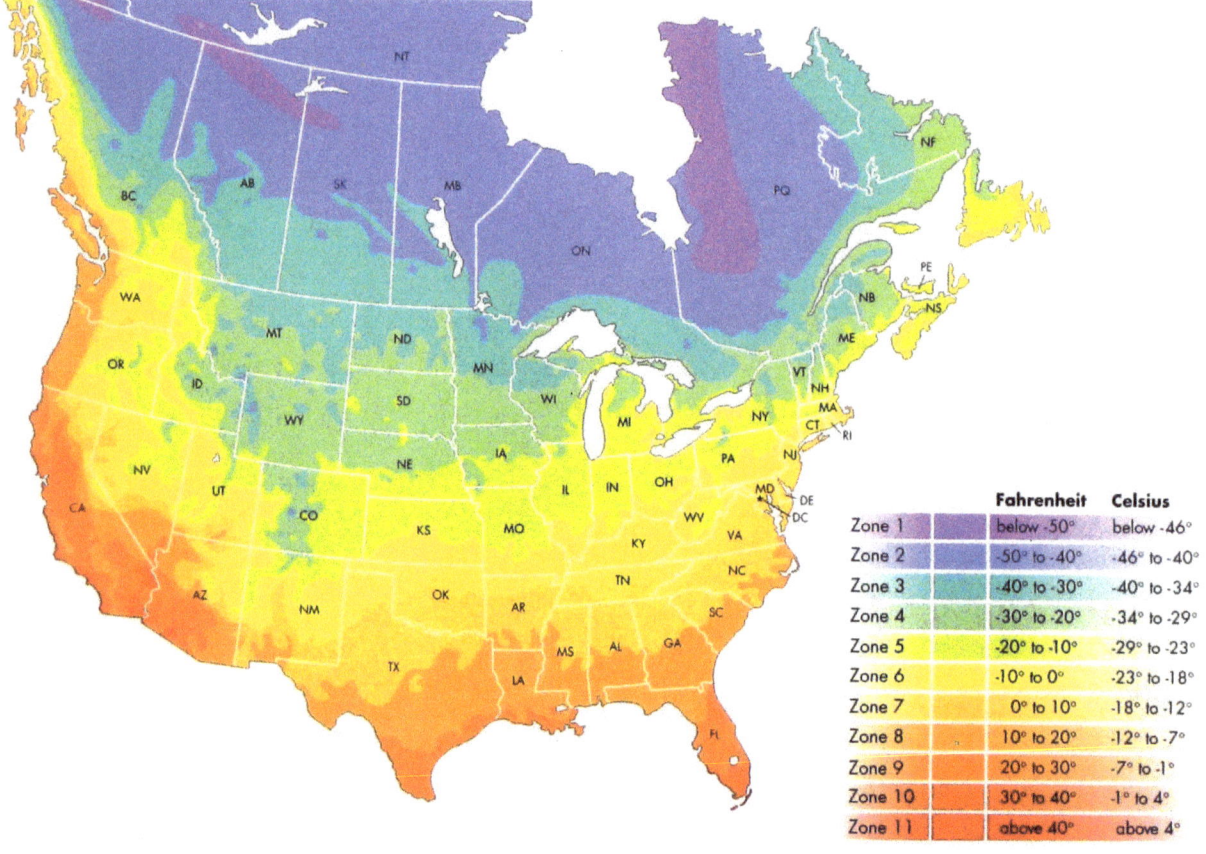

We live on Vancouver Island, B.C. If we waited until the first hard frost, it could be after Christmas, and almost time for me to be getting them waking up for the following year. As I sit here typing this manuscript, it is January 29th, and we have not had a hard frost yet and none in sight. We cut down on our schedule—October 1st every year—so they are all dug out at least before the heavy November rains start, which could mean we could lose stock in the ground to rot.

I generally have all the clumps split and labeled by the end of the first week of November, then stored away. In 2020, the rains started the first week of November, and we pretty much had rain daily for 28 days. This can be very typical on the West Coast.

My husband John is a huge help to me; I could not do what we have done without him. He digs out the 700 plus plants that we grow each year while I am busy splitting and labeling tubers. In addition, in the fall, John dresses all the beds with manure for the following spring and digs it under by hand.

Time for a much-needed glass of wine and feet up in front of the wood stove! I have already potted up about 275 tubers that I will be taking cuttings from. Our tubers have had over five months of growing time when we dig them out in the Fall.

LEAVING TUBERS PLANTED OVER WINTER

Not everyone can plant as early as late April. If you pre-start your tubers, you have at least a month or more of growing there—then add on three more months in the ground. This will help you figure out when you can cut them down and dig them out.

You might live in a climate where you can potentially leave tubers in the ground for the winter (zones 7, 7a, and 7b). Please know that you are taking a chance on losing them if you do not take precautions. This is a good time to decide how you will get them prepared to safely stay in the ground.

You can only do this in temperate climates that do not have heavy freezing. My best suggestion would be to cut them down to ground level, cover at least five to six inches with mulch or leaves, and then cover the whole bed with a large tarp. Put more mulch on that and some lumber on top to weigh the tarp down. This will provide protection for the plants. It is not necessary to cover the small open bits of the stalk; dahlia stalks have nodes built into them that control water. Just having the mulch and a tarp over them is all that is necessary.

It is the rains followed by a prolonged cold stretch that rots them in the ground. If you have well-drained soil, this can protect them. Leave this on top of the plants until your cold weather is done in the spring.

This method is not 100% guaranteed, but most people can save them this way in these growing zones.

WINTER *Storage*

ZONE 8 OR HIGHER

I suggest storing your tubers in the ground. You do not have cool enough conditions to store them out of the ground. You can lift in the spring, split your clumps, and allow the cuts to air-dry for 24 hours, then re-plant at that time.

ZONE 7-7A-7B

I suggest you dig them out if you have somewhere ideal to store them, split or whole, where you can store them at 38° F to 43° F where they cannot freeze. It also needs to be secure from rodents.

If you prefer to leave them in the ground, mulch five to six inches and cover with a tarp fastened down with logs, two-by-fours, etc. Winter rains plus some colder weather can rot them in the ground.

CONNIE THOMPSON

ZONE 6 AND LOWER

You clearly must dig out!

If you dig out and store WHOLE, **do not wash the dirt off**. Knock off the excess and cut the stalk down to one inch off the tubers, label, allow to dry for three to four days, and store them appropriate to your location. It is particularly important to cut that stalk off as much as possible. The old stalk can both mold and rot. This will be trial and error until you figure out what works best for your location and storage facility.

You will need somewhere the tubers cannot freeze—preferably at 38° F to 43° F—with reasonable humidity (70 percent is ideal) that's rodent-proof!

If you are in a location of HIGH HUMIDITY—the West Coast particularly—vermiculite is your best storage medium, in a plastic container with the lid not snapped shut. Vermiculite can be used year after year, and it does not support mold spores. You can store it for the summer in a tote or garbage can out in the heat and re-use it the following season.

You can try wood shavings, but they are prone to mold on the West (Wet) Coast. If you want to use wood shavings, try to get cedar shavings. I am not a fan of peat moss for storage unless you have IDEAL storage conditions because it is prone to mold unless you can store at 40° F on a consistent basis.

If you are in the Northern U.S. or Canada, or one of the many parts of the Central and Eastern Seaboard with sub-zero winter temperatures and LOW HUMIDITY, you can store in wood shavings or peat moss in a plastic container or bin. You might not have a place to store between 38° F to 43° F, but up to 50° F (or 10° C) will work.

Put a lid on your bin or container with the lid not clicked shut but shut enough to keep the moisture in the tubers so they do not get desiccated. You probably will not have a moisture problem or mold.

If you do not have an ideal spot to store your tubers, consider using Styrofoam coolers or an old freezer (that is not plugged in, of course!). Styrofoam coolers are readily available—thrift shops often have them, or your local pharmacy if you ask the shipper-receiver.

Storing your tubers in coolers keeps your tubers at a more or less constant temperature. If you do not have a good spot to keep them so they will not freeze, these coolers can be put in a cool storage room or un-heated room, so the tubers are not stored in your house and dry out.

Try to keep them off the cement floor, even if you put a couple of pieces of two by four under the bins—and **do not** store in the same room as your furnace!

Avoid using cardboard boxes, newspapers, or paper bags!! They all wick moisture from your tubers, and in humid areas are a recipe for MOLD…

Paper + Moisture + Warmth = Mold

OUR STORAGE AND WORK ROOM

We had this 12-by-20-foot insulated shed built about 10 years ago. It is fitted up with electricity and lots of plug outlets. The back and front walls, where I do my dahlia splitting, are pretty much floor-to-ceiling shelf and storage areas. Down the center of the room, I have a four-by-two-foot table and a large stainless rack. Further down the center, there is a nest of three 30-inch-wide storage racks.

This allows access to all areas, including across the middle of the room. It is tight but very functional, and I walk miles in there every spring putting dahlia tuber orders together. I have a telephone in there, a radio, good lights, and a bit of heat, as necessary.

I keep an oil-filled radiator-style electric heater in there for the winter months. We have a remote thermometer sensor in the house so we can check every evening on what the temperature is in the storage shed. We keep it 41° F to 45° F (5° C to 7° C).

For many months of the year, it is my 'home away from home,' as I spend six weeks in there in the fall splitting and storing tubers. In mid-January through to early April, I organize what we will grow and put together dahlia tuber orders that are shipped out later across Canada. In addition to this, I also pot up tubers that we grow on as plants for sale in late April. As I start working in there in mid-January, it feels cold, and I keep a small radiant heater on at my feet, so I do not turn into a popsicle!

I was told recently about a Bluetooth thermometer/hygrometer that gives readings for both temperature and humidity. They are available for roughly $15 US, and the brand name is Govee: they are available on-line.

SARAN WRAP METHOD OF STORAGE

This is a method of storing individual tubers wrapped tightly in Saran Wrap in small bundles and taped shut.

This method only works if you can keep the tubers at a constant cold temperature of 40° F. It is not recommended to store them in a refrigerator, as the newer 'Frost Free' refrigerators can remove the moisture out of the tubers. It would possibly be okay if you bundled them up into a plastic shoebox-sized storage bin with the lid on and stacked those up in your garage refrigerator if it is an older model. It is the constant cool temperature that is crucial. Using a cooler to store them in would work as well.

If your temperatures are all over the map like they are on the West Coast, I would not suggest this method. You will lose many of them to rot unless you have a way of keeping the temperature constant.

OKAY, WE HAVE THE STORAGE FACILITY ALL FIGURED OUT

IF YOU PLAN TO STORE YOUR CLUMPS WHOLE FOR THE WINTER, DO NOT TAKE THE DIRT OFF. Just knock off the excess, cut the old stalk off right down to just above the tubers, and let them dry for a few days, then store them.

If you put them in wood shavings or vermiculite in an open container, the tubers will dry out. If they are in a location where they are a bit warm, they could go soft and shrivel. If rodents have access to this space, they will have food for the winter months.

I suggest that you store them in a storage medium, completely covering them in your container, and then put the lid loosely on top. If you want to stack your containers, that is fine; if the lid is slightly askew or not snapped shut, they will still stack fine. It would be a good idea to put some mesh screen material on top of the storage medium to keep the mice out, though! Check them once a month while in storage.

Come spring, when you start to see the new eyes forming, you can split your clump into several pieces as you can easily see the eyes at this point.

IF YOU PLAN TO SPLIT YOUR TUBERS IN THE FALL, YOU NEED TO WASH THE CLUMPS. Allow them to air dry outside if possible, for the day, then split and label them. Allow the tubers to dry for two days further, then store them. You could use wood shavings or peat moss if you are in a cold location, or vermiculite if your winters are not cold. They should come out in the spring in excellent shape. Vermiculite for temperate areas works best, as it will not harbor mold spores, and wood shavings can. Vermiculite can be used every year, year after year, not so wood shavings which can not be used a 2nd year. **Vermiculite does not have asbestos in it anymore and is very safe for the horticultural industry to use.**

The ideal storage temperature is about 40° F, but if you are in a very cold location, you can store them a bit warmer since your humidity is probably extremely low. I can store between 40° F and 43° F with a humidity level of about 75 percent. We store exclusively in vermiculite, and the tubers come out like carrots out of the fridge in the spring.

Storing them in a plastic container is best. If you are using a large Rubbermaid-type bin, I would drill small three-eighth-inch holes up the sides on the lower part of the bin to allow excess moisture to escape. If you use small shoebox-size storage containers, this is not normally necessary—just do not snap the lid closed unless you can store them very cool—48° F to 43° F.

SPLITTING *your Dahlia tubers in the fall*

GETTING STARTED WITH SPLITTING

If you are doing FALL SPLITTING, **do not dig the entire garden at the same time.** The tubers will be getting soft and dried-out before you finish splitting. <u>Dig out what you feel you can comfortably split within two days, then dig again.</u> This way, your tubers will go into storage nice and firm and plump and should come out like carrots in the spring.

You will be amazed at the growth that a single tuber can make in one growing season. Five to 10 tubers in the fall from one planted in the spring is to be expected.

The clumps are easier to split in the fall, and the clumps are much tougher to split in spring—BUT, if you do not know what you are looking for, it is easier to see the eyes in the spring.

I have put together a PHOTOGRAPHIC TUTORIAL on **Connie's Dahlias** (my Facebook page) that will help you through this, with information on every photo. You're welcome to visit it for reference to get you through this task! It is also on many different Dahlias sites.

Remember, the next year's eyes will form where the tuber attaches to the old stalk. They look like emerging 'pimples' in the fall and can be pale yellow, pale green, and in some cases more pinkish.

All viable tubers will be directly attached to the old stock. The new growth for the following season comes from this area. Tubers 'growing from tubers' never produce eyes—they can be removed, as there is no point storing something that won't grow.

Tubers that have a 'neck' less than the diameter of a pencil will probably dry out in storage. I would leave tubers like this in a small clump or with another more viable tuber. Remember, eyes form where the tubers attach to the stalk—they never form at the bottom of the tuber where the roots are or along the sides of a tuber.

If you plan to split your tubers in the fall, here is a list of tools that I use every year to do this huge chore:

- FELCO #2 cutters
- bonsai scissors (I like eight-and-a-half-inch ones, as they are easier on the hands. They are extremely sharp, so be careful not to stab yourself or cut your other hand!)
- a strong, sturdy knife, like a hunting knife
- dust brush
- old toothbrush

These are my main tools as I split dahlias. If I have a particularly difficult clump, I also use a pair of loppers for a thick stalk.

Some clumps are a large mess of tubers that makes you wonder how to approach it. In this case, cut off the stalk down to the top of the tubers and cut off all the roots. Then, with a sturdy knife, turn the clump upside down so it's resting on the old stalk and split it down the middle, so you have two pieces. Know that you will probably lose a couple in the process but will gain more for doing this. You can repeat this process if it is a particularly large clump. If you are unsure of where to split the tubers further, store these pieces until spring. You will be able to see the eyes much easier at this point, and if the clump needs to be split down further, you can.

Just remember that you must have an 'eye' with each tuber for it to grow.

QUESTIONS That I often get from people...

Can I grow more of my favorite variety by collecting seeds from my favorite plant?

NO. Dahlias only grow true by propagating from tubers or cuttings from a tuber.

If I grow from dahlia seeds, will they look like the parents?

NO. Dahlias are 'octoploids:' they have a complex gene system, and every seed will make a 'new variety,' so to speak. This is how hybridizers develop new varieties; by taking select seeds from dahlia parents that they know to be good seed parents and sometimes growing thousands of seeds every summer. Then, they choose quality blooms that meet their criteria to grow again the following year. Many of these seedlings will appear with missing petals and misshapen blooms that are not worth saving. But out of, say, 100 seedling plants you have something you like, grow it again as it can improve in year two and three! A good hybridizer will often grow that seedling for three to seven years before releasing that new variety to the public when they know it is stabilized.

What are these white dots on my dahlia tubers? Is this a disease? Do I need to throw them out?

NO, and NO to both questions! Those small white dots on your tubers are called LENTICILS. They are like open pores on your skin from being in too much wet soil. They will not affect the tubers at all for growing next season!

How many blooms can I expect on my plants?

Depending on the variety, you can expect to have from eight to 12 blooms (giant sizes eight to 10 inches and larger) to over 100 blooms (pompon varieties that are under two inches in diameter) per tuber planted in the summer. To ensure continuous blooming from August until frost, REMOVE all dead blossoms as soon as they have 'blown' their centers and you can see the pollen. (This would be for fully double blooms.) If you do not deadhead regularly from all types of dahlias, the plant will think that it has finished blooming for the season and eventually will stop making new growth.

For floral arrangements and bouquets, cut flowers from your garden either early in the morning or late in the day directly into a bucket of two inches of clean, very warm (100° F) water. Put your blooms into the bucket directly as you cut and leave them in this for half an hour, then place them in cold water. This will hydrate them. If displayed in a cool part of the house (not in direct sunlight) and the water in the vase is changed daily, the flowers, once cut and hydrated, will last about a week. Ball and formal decorative dahlias under six inches in diameter will last longer in a vase than other types, such as cactus, and more loose and open types of dahlias. Blooms over eight inches in diameter generally only last one to three days at best. You will get longer lasting blooms if you use Floralife in your cutting water and in your vases. Packages of Floralife are readily available on the internet.

DAHLIA PESTS
that we all have to deal with

SLUGS AND SLUG BAIT TRAPS

Slugs love to feast on dahlias—particularly the leaves. You can get on top of these in a couple of ways. Pest control is diverse when dealing with slugs.

- Use cream cheese or sour cream containers with a bit of beer in them and place them on the ground near each plant. They love beer and will crawl in there and drink it and die.
- Use diatomaceous earth or crushed eggshells around each plant at ground level. The slugs usually will not go over either one. If you get rains, you will have to sprinkle more diatomaceous earth.
- Use a ring of copper wire or metal strips as this will electrocute them.
- Cut the bottom out of a 1-gallon pot and place this 'collar' over your young dahlia plants.

APHIDS

There are both green and black aphids, and these are usually 'farmed by ants' on dahlia stalks. There could be hundreds of them on a plant. You need to deal with both the aphids and the ants every year, early on. On Vancouver Island, British Columbia, I can usually plant by the third week in April, and I start dealing with both often within the following weeks from planting.

For aphids, if you only have a few plants, you can religiously wash off the aphids, but you will have to do it pretty much daily. Instead, I suggest you spray them with a mix of a few squirts of Dawn dish soap and a few drops of cooking oil in a bottle of water. Spray as often as you see them and try to get them off the plants in the process.

Another option is to order beneficial predators from a company that provides them. This is the route that we go: with over 700 dahlias in the ground, I would be spraying 24/7 and do not have that kind of time. We use a beneficial predator called APHIDOLETES. They are a midge that comes in a container of bran meal. You merely sprinkle it on the foliage and ground around your plants and let them go to work and control the aphids.

We also order several thousand native ladybugs and let them loose in our garden. Ladybugs that are not native to your area just leave in a day or two.

It is vital that you control aphids, as they bring viruses to your garden. Mosaic virus is one of the worst that can infect your dahlias and they will not grow properly at all. (More about this later.) They will have yellow along the veins of the foliage, and your plants will be short and stunted. If you find mosaic virus, remove the plant and get rid of it in your garbage.

THRIPS

These little creatures love to chew your plants and can pass bacterial infections between dahlias and many other virus-host plants, like weeds! Again, these can be controlled by regularly spraying every couple of days, or you can introduce beneficial predators to your garden. We use one called CUCUMERIS that also comes in a container of bran. I like to get these on by early May before it starts to heat up and we have a problem! This needs to be done yearly.

If you do not control them, pests can destroy your plants over the summer growing season. You would see wrinkled foliage and plants that are really struggling.

WIREWORM

Wireworms are endemic in North America and horrible to deal with in a dahlia garden. They are the larvae stage of the **Click Beetle**, and you need to deal with all stages of this creature to get them under control. They love to burrow into dahlia tubers, especially where the growth starts at the top of the tuber and can kill a tuber in the process.

We have learned a lot about control with them in the past few years. We initially 'seeded' our dahlia beds in the early spring with chunks of potato with a long cable tie pushed through it and planted a few inches into the soil. The wireworms are attracted to them. Do this before you plant! Then, dig the chunks of potato out every few days; they will be loaded with wireworms. Toss them into a garbage bag and get rid of them. There are lots more of them in the soil yet!

The other way we have dealt with them is to hand-pick them out of the dirt, break them into two pieces, then stomp on them.

Since then, we have had an entomologist here, and she suggested that we plant a cover crop in February each year of WHITE MUSTARD SEED. Before it is planting time, mow it down and then dig it under or rototill it into your soil. It is a natural deterrent for the wireworm, and since using it for the first-time last spring, we saw hardly any of them this past summer. It grows extremely fast and within two months of planting is ready to cut. You could also Fall sow and it would get winter kill and the roots that are the deterrent would possibly still be in the soil in the Spring.

They have destroyed far too many of our tubers over the years!

Click beetles are the adult version of the wireworm that like to live in the grassy areas around your dahlia beds. It lays its eggs in the grass that will become juvenile wireworms that you can treat with beneficial nematodes available at most nurseries. The click beetles can be treated with SEVIN on all the grassy areas adjoining your dahlia beds, if you still have access to it. Sevin is now banned in Canada.

The juvenile wireworms are about a quarter of an inch long and translucent. Watering in beneficial nematodes will take care of them at this stage but will not deal with the larvae stage when they are yellow in color.

OTHER PESTS

You might see whiteflies, green lacewings, or other pests. Some of them are a problem, and some are going after the other pests already there. Research and get to know what they look like. You do not want to be spraying creatures that are doing good in your garden.

Japanese Beetles is another pest that we do not have here yet. Many people are ordering in organza bags the size of their blooms and covering the buds before the beetles destroy them. Hand picking them off your plants into a bucket of soapy water is probably the surest method. So far, I have not seen a spray that deals with them without killing everything in your garden.

DAHLIA
Diseases

There are many diseases that can affect dahlias, but the primary ones are the following:

LEAFY GALL

Leafy gall will have a proliferation of flat, fused eyes or sprouts that produce many skinny 'stalks,' and your plant will flower but never properly. Leafy gall is a BACTERIAL infection that is carried in the tubers, and there is **NO CURE** for this. It gets spread through not cleaning your tools regularly, and also through watering, as it can travel the same path as the water's course.

These plants need to be culled and put in your garbage or your burn pile if you have one, NOT your compost.

Make sure to clean any tools that you use with your dahlias regularly in a 10 percent bleach solution, then wash the bleach off (as it is corrosive on metal tools).

You cannot just cut out the infected area and plant the rest of the tubers; the entire clump is infected with these bacteria. Once the infected clump is dug out, the bacteria does not last long in the soil.

There is considerable research being done on gall diseases in general and how they affect your soil. From what I have read, the bacteria does not survive in the soil awfully long, and it would be dead long before the next planting season. This information still needs to be confirmed and the research continues. This disease, according to the research that has been done, is largely transmitted by cutting tools, much as viruses like mosaic are transmitted. However, to clarify the difference, the mosaic virus (and other viruses that can attack dahlias) is not transmitted by water. Contaminated water in your flower beds does spread leafy gall disease. This is the difference.

CROWN GALL

Crown gall will exhibit as small spheres or growths where the tubers attach to the old stalk, or large growths just about anywhere on the tubers or clumps of tubers. This is also a nasty bacterial infection that you do not want in your garden. There is no cure for this infection. It is carried within the tubers, not in the soil, and once the 'host' plant is removed, it will not last long in your soil. You cannot just cut off the growth and plant tubers that 'are not affected;' the entire clump is carrying the bacteria.

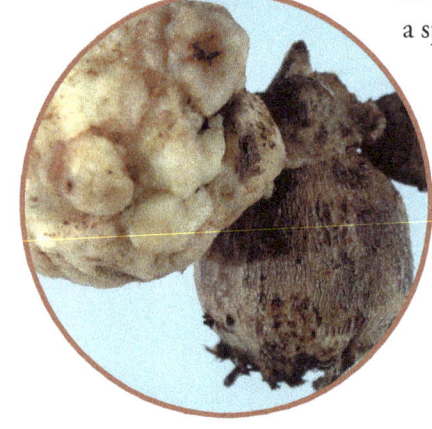

Tubers that are infected with crown gall usually never produce 'eyes' to make a sprout.

Destroy in your garbage or on a burn pile, do not put on your compost, and CLEAN all your tools with a 10 percent bleach solution, then wash them, as bleach is hard on tools.

The photo I have shown you shows a small Gall, but they can vary from growths the size of a marble to the size of your hand on tubers. As the bacterium is carried within the tubers you can not just remove the area with the Gall and plant the remainder. The entire clump is infected.

MOSAIC VIRUS

This virus is often introduced into your garden by insects chewing on your dahlias after visiting other gardens where the virus is present. Aphids and thrips are certainly two regular culprits! It can also arrive in plants that you get from other people's gardens.

Control these pests, and you probably will not see it. The virus is pretty much obvious in the foliage of the plants, and you can see it with yellowing along the veins of the leaves and short plants that are not growing properly.

Dig out plants that are exhibiting mosaic virus and dispose of them in your garbage. Clean your tools! There is lots of information and photos of mosaic virus online.

A combination of virus-free stock and rigorous disinfecting practices on your tools can produce an extremely low incidence of the virus in your garden. Until sources of clean stock become more readily available, it is especially important that you retain only the healthiest-looking plants for future stock.

If in doubt about whether you have it, throw it out. But be aware that there are many other reasons for yellowing that are often associated with lack of poor nutrients, which then affects the plant's ability to take up what it needs for photosynthesis. There is an excellent document available on yellowing dahlias leaves that is certainly worth reading. Please see the Resource Page for more information.

LEAF MINERS

There is an excellent document available on leaf miners on dahlias that I recommend that you familiarize yourself with. You do not see them often, but they do show up from time to time. Please see the Resource Page for further information. As this is something that we have not seen before, I do not have a photo to present here.

RESOURCE PAGE

- More information on yellowing on dahlia leaves:

https://www.gardeningknowhow.com/ornamental/bulbs/dahlia/yellow-dahlia-foliage.htm

- More information on leaf miners:

https://www.gardeningknowhow.com/plant-problems/pests/insects/leaf-miner-control.

- Pentel N50 markers are available on Amazon.

GENERAL INFORMATION

- You might consider joining your local Dahlia Society affiliated with the American Dahlia Society at https://www.dahlia.org or the Federation of Northwest Dahlias Growers at www.nwdahlia.org. This is a wonderful way to get information from experienced growers who are only too eager to help new growers. You will find one in most major cities in Canada and the U.S.
- There is also lots of information on the internet on pretty much every aspect of growing and storing dahlias for different areas of the continent. ***NOTE: some of it is correct and some of it is not. There are a few too many old wives' tales still floating around out there!***
- My favorite resource would be the American Dahlia Society website—it is readily available and is a huge resource for any dahlia grower. I have been a member for over 30 years, and as a member I have access to other parts of the site that other visitors to the site would not be able to access.
- I receive a classification handbook of varieties every year, and quarterly bulletins full of interesting information on growing. Out of choice, I pay as a family so that I get two copies of the classification book, one for the house and one for my tuber shed. It is an excellent investment, and I have https://www.gardeningknowhow.com/ornamental/bulbs/dahlia/yellow-dahlia-foliage.htmlearned a lot over the years. The cost to join and get a classification book and quarterly editions of the bulletin with tons of interesting information is approximately $27–30 USD for family. It is slightly higher in Canada.
- You can also find lots of this information on Connie's Dahlias on Facebook—in the photo area you will find albums with step-by-step information on many aspects of growing dahlias through each season. https://www.facebook.com/Connies.Dahlias

ACKNOWLEDGEMENT PAGE

PHOTO CREDIT: Karen Bull, my dear friend

Enjoy your wonderful blooms—I certainly know that I do!

I am a smaller commercial grower on the west coast of Canada and have been growing dahlias for over 30 years. I have been trained as a dahlia judge through the American Dahlia Society and have been a member since 1989.

For many years I have been compiling and researching information that would help the newer dahlia grower get started with confidence. I hope that you find this book useful in helping you with day-to-day information on growing dahlias. It has been a pleasure for me to put this information together for you.

When I think back on all the Senior Judges that I have had the privilege of working with over the years, it makes me sad so many of them are gone today. They were just the best resource for information and taught me so very much.

CPSIA information can be obtained
at www.ICGtesting.com
Printed in the USA
LVHW070122261021
701557LV00013B/712